In the sun.

Story written by Gill Munton
Illustrated by Tim Archbold

Speed Sounds

Consonants   *Ask children to say the sounds.*

f	l	m	n	r	s	v	z	**sh**	**th**	**ng**
ff	**ll**		**nn**	rr	ss	ve	zz			**nk**
	le		kn				s			

b	c	d	g	h	j	p	qu	t	w	x	y	**ch**
bb	k	dd	gg			p	pp		tt	wh			tch
	ck											

Each box contains one sound but sometimes more than one grapheme.
*Focus graphemes for this story are **circled**.*

Vowels

Ask children to say the sounds in and out of order.

a	e	i	o	u	ay	ee	igh	ow
	ea					y		
at	hen	in	on	up	day	see	high	blow

oo	oo	ar	or	air	ir	ou	oy
zoo	look	car	for	fair	whirl	shout	boy

Story Green Words

Ask children to read the words first in Fred Talk and then say the word.

flag   jam   frock   blob   stuff   rug   mug

Mr Punch

Ask children to say the syllables and then read the whole word.

buck|et   funn|y   lol|ly   com|ic

Ask children to read the root first and then the whole word with the suffix.

shell → shells   crisp → crisps

splash → splashing   shrimp → shrimps

crab → crabs   smell → smells

6

Red Words

Ask children to practise reading the words across the rows, down the columns and in and out of order clearly and quickly.

my	of	the	your
all	call	want	no
we	her	he	to
I've	are	said	go

In the sun

Soft wet sand,
a bucket in my hand.

Shrimps and crabs and shells,
funny fishy smells.

A ship with a flag,
yummy crisps in a bag.

Red jam in a bun,
a comic in the sun.

A can full of pop,
a net from the shop.

A stick of pink rock,
Mr Punch in his frock.

Splashing Dad and Mum,
a blob of sun stuff on my tum.

A lolly on the rug,
and milk in a mug.

I had such a lot of fun
with Mum and Dad
in the sun.

Questions to talk about

Ask children to TTYP for each question using 'Fastest finger' (FF) or 'Have a think' (HaT).

p.8 (FF) How does Meg describe the sand?

p.9 (FF) What can Meg smell?

p.10 (FF) What does she eat while she reads her comic in the sun?

p.11 (HaT) Who is Mr Punch?

p.12 (FF) What does Meg do to Dad and Mum?

p.13 (FF) How do we know Meg enjoyed her day?